IMAGES

Red

Karen Bryant-Mole

Heinemann

First published in Great Britain by Heinemann Library, an imprint of
Heinemann Publishers (Oxford) Ltd, Halley Court, Jordan Hill, Oxford OX2 8EJ

MADRID ATHENS PARIS FLORENCE PRAGUE WARSAW
PORTSMOUTH NH CHICAGO SAO PAULO SINGAPORE TOKYO
MELBOURNE AUCKLAND IBADAN GABORONE JOHANNESBURG

Designed by Jean Wheeler
Commissioned photography by Zul Mukhida
Printed in Hong Kong

00 99 98 97 96
10 9 8 7 6 5 4 3 2 1

ISBN 0 431 06279 X

British Library Cataloguing in Publication Data
Bryant-Mole, Karen
  Red. – (Images Series)
  I. Title II. Series
  535.6

**Some of the more difficult words in this book are
explained in the glossary.**

Acknowledgements
The Publishers would like to thank the following for permission to reproduce photographs. Chapel Studios; 8 (right) Oliver
Cockell, Houses and Interiors; 8 (left) Peter Etchells, 9 (right) Gordon L Wigens, Oxford Scientific Films; 9 (left) Geoff Kidd,
17 (right) Alan Root, Tony Stone Images; 16 (left) Tom Tietz, 17 (left) Rosemary Calvert, 22 (right) Vince Streano,
Zefa; 16 (right), 22 (left), 23 (both).

Every effort has been made to contact copyright holders of any material reproduced in this book. Any omissions will be
rectified in subsequent printings if notice is given to the Publisher.

Contents

Toys

a red plane

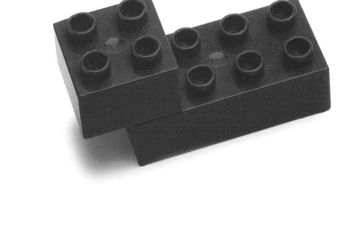

a red car

some red bricks

a red yo-yo

a red crab

5

Party-time

Lots of parties are
birthday parties.

Have you been
to a birthday
party?

Flowers

Can you find out which of these flowers is called a rose?

Bed-time

A soft toy feels
nice to cuddle
in bed.

11

Clothes

Clothes like these are useful on a cold day.

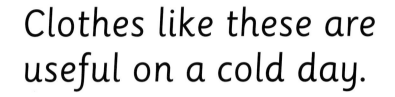

13

On the beach

spade

bucket

rake

sand
moulds

hat

A hat will
protect your
head from
the hot sun.

Animal world

a bird

some fish

some insects

a mammal

In the kitchen

All these things belong in the kitchen.

What are they used for?

Fruit

sweet
strawberries

crunchy
apples

juicy plums

This tomato
is a fruit, too.

On the move

a ship

a bus

a helicopter

a truck

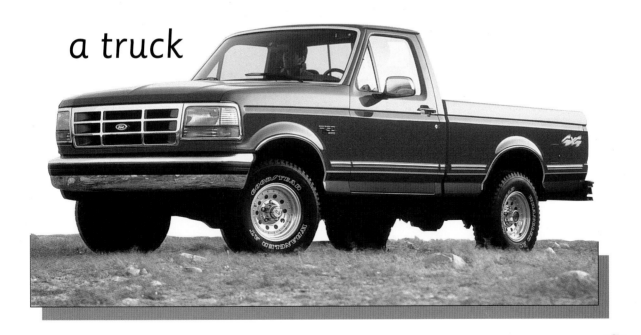

Glossary

insect a small animal with six legs
mammal an animal with warm blood that
   feeds its young with milk
moulds used to make things like sand or
   food into a special shape
protect keep safe

Index